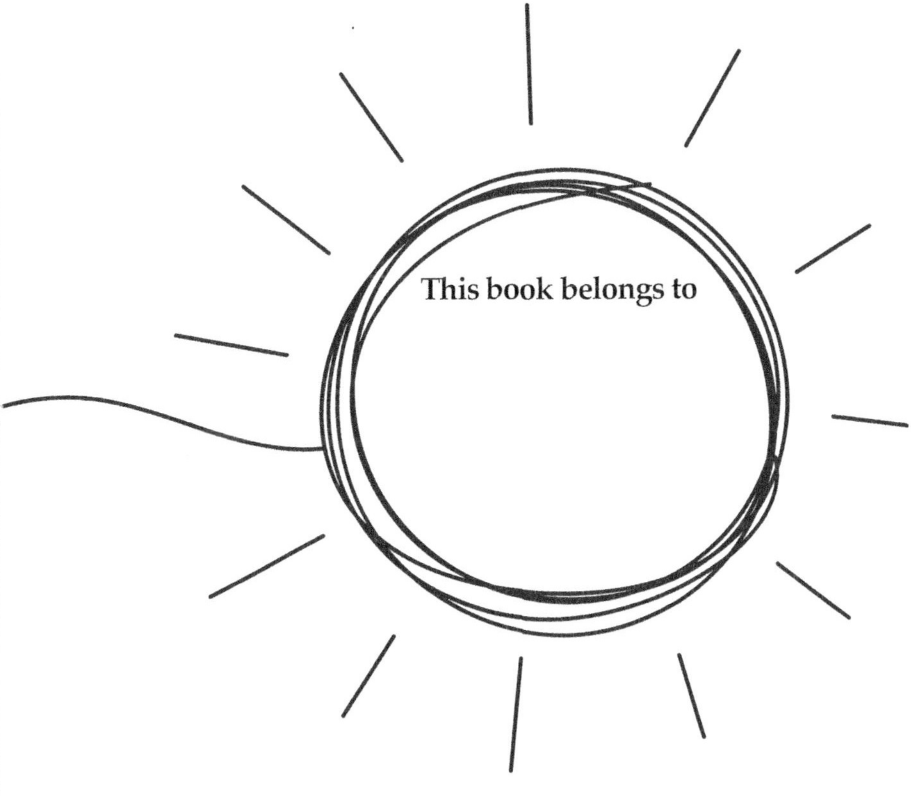
This book belongs to

ALSO BY DAVID LOWE

The Innovation Revelation: A story about how to satisfy customer needs

The Lemonade Stall: How to test and validate ideas

Scrum 101: The most frequently asked questions about Agile with Scrum

You're on Mute! Facilitating online workshops with a touch of fun

COACHING JOURNAL

A GUIDE AND JOURNAL

DAVID LOWE

First Edition

Manufactured in the United Kingdom. ISBN: 978-1-9162446-5-8

Created with Vellum

For all my clients

In memory of Doug Nicoll

(1979-2020)

FOREWORD

Even after more of a decade of professional practice, I continue to be fascinated by the deceptive simplicity of coaching. By holding the space for another, we create the conditions for a deep exploration of experience, generating new awareness and learning, and supporting positive actions as a result. We are required to be fully present with our client, dancing in the moment, reacting spontaneously, being curious and trusting our gut reactions. However, we are also listening at many levels, noticing what is happening in the relationship between us, noting trends, patterns and absences. We develop a cumulative understanding of our client over many sessions. This multi-level awareness drives our contribution to the relationship so that we can be a true thinking partner.

It would be asking too much of even the most skilled reflexive practitioner to be able to capture every possibility in the moment. This is why I believe that the reflective practice outside of sessions that this Coaching Journal provides is invaluable.

Developmental psychologist Robert Kegan said that humans are meaning making machines. We can't help but make meaning from our experiences. But all too often this process happens too quickly, before we have examined enough evidence. The 'what happened?' section of the reflective templates in this book will help you slow down and get back to the things themselves. By delaying our meaning making, we allow more evidence to emerge.

Then the 'so what?' section gives space for unnoticed patterns, new insights and alternative interpretations to emerge. The additional insights emerging from this process can be multifaceted. You may achieve new insights about the client, their context, your relationship or yourself.

The 'now what?' question prompts us to do something useful with our insights. I have often found that taking those insights back into the next conversation has uncovered a crucial developmental opportunity. It's also been enormously helpful to take a concise summary of my reflections into a supervision session to get to the heart of the matter quickly.

I wish you joy in using this book. Allow yourself to be you, with all your qualities, strengths and deficits. And do it with compassion and hope. We all are, and will always be, becoming the reflective practitioner we wish to be.

Linda Spencer

Creative Vectors Ltd.

www.CreativeVectorsCoaching.co.uk

Linda entered the world of coaching following a successful international career in the automotive industry. With a MA in Coaching and Mentoring Practice, published research and the experience of working with more than 500 clients internationally, she enjoys being a thinking partner for clients who want to improve their leadership and create positive change in their personal and professional lives.

WHAT IS JOURNALLING?

> *A vehicle for reflection.*
>
> JENNIFER A. MOON

Journalling is writing down what happened in a coaching (or mentoring or teaching or facilitation or whatever) session.

But it is much more than a mere log of events; as well as recording what happened, we analyse and interpret events in order to make sense of them. This helps us challenge our thinking and, in turn, learn from our actions and develop our practice.

In short, it is a method of helping us improve.

WHY SHOULD I DO IT?

> *A beginner learns the theory.*
>
> *A practitioner puts theory into effect.*
>
> *An expert regularly reflects upon their performance.*
>
> DAVID LOWE

Theoretical knowledge is a foundation for coaching but is not enough; one must have practical, hands-on experience. But this is not enough either: one must reflect on one's performance to appreciate what has happened.

My view of the world, when it comes to coaching, is that reality is what we perceive it to be; there is not one objective reality or truth to be uncovered. For example, I may find a comment made by a client to be humorous, but that doesn't mean it *is* funny; just that *I* perceived it to be funny. Journaling helps us create, identify and label our reality.

In turn, this helps us grow. Journalling, like coaching, helps provoke thought, inspire us, unlock our potential, overcome challenges, reach goals and find fulfilment (yes, they are points pulled from the International Coaching Federation's definition of coaching). I'd say it also helps inspect attitudes, beliefs and assumptions as well as interpretations.

For example, my musings on my coaching practice has helped me challenge my self-doubt and imposter syndrome. The process of digging into my practice helped me spot recurring patterns, such as the fact that, although I kept many of my failures in perspective, I played down my successes. In addition, it helped me notice patterns in some of my clients too.

One final reason for journalling is that it helps maintain enthusiasm. Learning and development is tough. Like everyone else, I hit a point in my studies where I ask "Why the hell am I doing this?!". At these moments, journalling is there to help me persevere.

DO I DO IT ALONE?

> How many coaches does it take to change a lightbulb?
>
> One, but the lightbulb has to want to change.

It's an old joke, but it reminds us that you, and only you, are responsible for the change you hope to achieve. I suspect that you, like me, have embarked upon a significant process of learning and development. Journalling allows us to take ownership of our actions and move towards our goals.

However, saying that, journalling is a great source of material for you to take to mentor coaching and coaching supervision.

HOW DO I DO IT?

I was introduced to the work of Terry Borton through Gary Rolfe, Dawn Freshwater and Melanie Jasper's book, *Critical reflection for nursing and the helping professions: a user's guide*. They built upon Borton's model, connecting it with others' work, to create a reflective model centred around three questions: What? So what? Now what? I have borrowed bits from them and others (see acknowledgements) for you to use in your journalling.

Each reflection is split into three stages:

What happened? This is where you describe what happened from your own subjective perspective.

So what? This is where you consider what impact the event has had on you.

Now what? This is where you consider what action you will take as a result of having reflected on it?

. . .

Consider each stage of your session and think about what you and your client said, felt, did, thought, etc. I have supplied some thought-provoking questions for each stage below (and as a pull-out version at the back of the book for easy reference). You don't have to answer each question. Do what works for you. I have also included an example at the start of the journal section.

What happened?

- What did you do and say? What did they do and say?
- What else did you notice? (paraverbal, non-verbal, expressions)
- What went well? What did not go so well?
- What did you want to happen? How did what happened differ from your expectations?
- What was your role?
- How did you feel? How do you think they felt?
- What did they want/need/expect from you?
- Was what you did appropriate? Was what they did appropriate?

So what?

- Why did you act in the way you did?
- How do your past experiences relate to what happened?
- What beliefs or assumptions were involved?
- How did your/their behaviour fit with your values?
- How have your views changed?
- What are the consequences?
- How do you feel about it now? Why do you feel like this?
- What other options did you have?
- What have you learned?
- What would you keep and what would you change?
- What else is going on?
- In hindsight, what do you think you should have done?
- So what does this mean to you as a person/as a coach?

Now what?

- What do you want to do about it?
- What is the plan?
- What is the first step?
- What is the timescale for your actions?
- What do you think will happen if you take those actions?
- What action do you need to take for other clients too?
- What is the right thing to do?
- What could you do differently if in the same situation again?

Apparently the process of writing down your thoughts allows you to be more contemplative and a better problem-solver, as well as aiding recollection and memory. But journalling doesn't have to be words; you can include diagrams, sketches or even objects. Grab that sticky note and pop it in the book. Or a bus ticket. Or a leaf that fell while you were contemplating the session.

WHEN DO I DO IT?

If you are a practising coach, then I recommend you write in your journal after each session. It doesn't have to be immediately afterwards, but I have found it best to write up the 'What happened?' section as soon as possible after the session. Sometimes leaving a gap before answering the latter two questions helps; other times it means I forget to do it.

Many coaches recommend making journalling a pattern, such as writing in the same location, in the same book, at the same time, etc. If you find that you are short of time, you could write bullet points so you record the key events of a session.

I don't know what will work best for you so I suggest that you try a few different approaches to find out.

In addition to the standard three questions, from time to time I will throw in some more general contemplative questions around themes, patterns and even some existential ones!

FINALLY...

Be kind to yourself..

Not every reflection needs to result in a jaw-dropping revelation; record whatever comes to mind and has meaning to you. Improving through journalling is a gradual process, with every reflection helping you adapt, evolve, improve.

WANT MORE?

Go to https://davidlowe.coach/publications/coaching-journal/

Name: Bob

What happened?

EXAMPLE

Date: 13 March

Location: London HQ

Bob acknowledged he hadn't completed any of the actions he'd committed to in the previous session. He didn't seem that bothered and laughed it off. Prolonged eye contact was weird. Bob moved on quickly to a new topic and I didn't challenge him on his lack of action. I wanted him to talk about why he'd done nothing. Now I think about it, this lack of progress isn't unusual: he's committed to lots in previous sessions and hasn't done them either.

I thought I would have challenged him - isn't that part of my role?

I felt weak, unprofessional, uncomfortable and frustrated. I think Bob was embarrassed but I'm not sure. I realise that I don't know what Bob wants from me.

Prev session: 27 Feb

Next session: 28 Mar

So what?

I think I was scared to challenge Bob because he's a senior leader and has significant influence on future business. However, Bob has referred many people already, with no sign unhappy. No other clients have objected when I challenge. Bit of imposter syndrome and I wonder whether some perfectionism going on too? Achievement is a core value of mine, which maybe I'm transferring to Bob? I still feel it was wrong not to challenge Bob. I can only think of 2 options still: challenge or not challenge (I suppose there's different ways to challenge though).

EXAMPLE

Now what?

I am going to raise this with Bob in our next session (regardless of whether he has completed this session's actions).

- If he didn't complete: ask him what's going on (politely) → then may discuss whether he'd like me to hold him to account moving forwards
- If completed: ask about holding accountable.

If I do in my usual style, think will increase respect/trust.
Consider recontracting if necessary.
Lesson for future: Make sure I address accountability at start.
Take scenario to next supervision (esp. imp. syndrome)

Name:

Date:

Location:

What happened?

Prev session

Next session

So what?

Now what?

Name:

Date:

Location:

What happened?

Prev session

Next session

So what?

Now what?

Name:

Date:

Location:

What happened?

Prev session

Next session

So what?

Now what?

Name:

Date:

Location:

What happened?

Prev session

Next session

So what?

Now what?

Name:

Date:

Location:

What happened?

Prev session

Next session

So what?

Now what?

I don't focus on what I'm up against. I focus on my goals and I try to ignore the rest.

Venus Williams

What are your aims? What do you hope to achieve in both your life and your work?

Name:

Date:

Location:

What happened?

Prev session

Next session

So what?

Now what?

Name:

Date:

Location:

What happened?

Prev session

Next session

So what?

Now what?

Name:

Date:

Location:

What happened?

Prev session

Next session

So what?

Now what?

Name:

Date:

Location:

What happened?

Prev session

Next session

So what?

Now what?

Name:

Date:

Location:

What happened?

Prev session

Next session

So what?

Now what?

The future ain't what it used to be.

Yogi Berra

Write a letter to the future you.
You decide how far in the future you will be.

Name:

Date:

Location:

What happened?

Prev session

Next session

So what?

Now what?

Name:

Date:

Location:

What happened?

Prev session

Next session

So what?

Now what?

Name:

Date:

Location:

What happened?

Prev session

Next session

So what?

Now what?

Name:

Date:

Location:

What happened?

Prev session

Next session

So what?

Now what?

Name:

Date:

Location:

What happened?

Prev session

Next session

So what?

Now what?

All I know is what I read in the papers.

Will Rogers

You've hit the headlines!

What would the article be about? Fill in the template below.

There are spaces for a headline, a picture (black box), the text (right-hand side) and a call-out box (grey box) for anything else you want to add.

Name:

Date:

Location:

What happened?

Prev session

Next session

So what?

Now what?

Name:

Date:

Location:

What happened?

Prev session

Next session

So what?

Now what?

Name:

Date:

Location:

What happened?

Prev session

Next session

So what?

Now what?

Name:

Date:

Location:

What happened?

Prev session

Next session

So what?

Now what?

Name:

What happened?

Date:

Location:

Prev session

Next session

So what?

Now what?

Poetry is language at its most distilled and most powerful.

Rita Dove

Write a poem about your practice.

Name:

Date:

Location:

What happened?

Prev session

Next session

So what?

Now what?

Name:

Date:

Location:

What happened?

Prev session

Next session

So what?

Now what?

Name:

What happened?

Date:

Location:

Prev session

Next session

So what?

Now what?

Name:

Date:

Location:

What happened?

Prev session

Next session

So what?

Now what?

Name:

Date:

Location:

What happened?

Prev session

Next session

So what?

Now what?

The purpose of art is washing the dust of daily life off our souls.

Complete the drawing to identify what skills and competencies you have, which approaches you use and what techniques you like using.

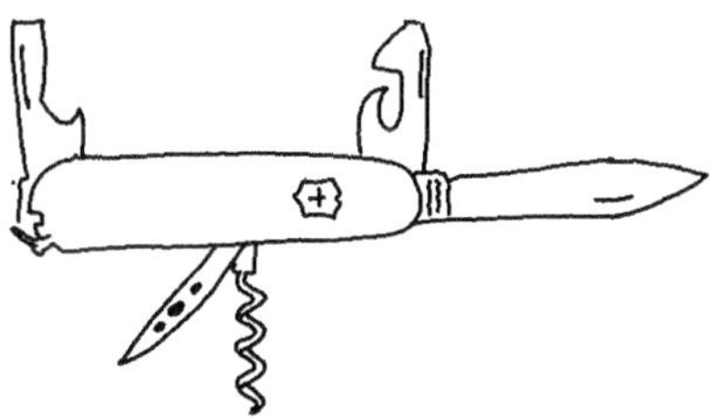

Name:

What happened?

Date:

Location:

Prev session

Next session

So what?

Now what?

Name:

Date:

Location:

What happened?

Prev session

Next session

So what?

Now what?

Name:

What happened?

Date:

Location:

Prev session

Next session

So what?

Now what?

Name:

What happened?

Date:

Location:

Prev session

Next session

So what?

Now what?

Name:

Date:

Location:

What happened?

Prev session

Next session

So what?

Now what?

Your assumptions are your windows on the world. Scrub them off every once in a while, or the light won't come in.

Isaac Asimov

What assumptions do you make about your clients?

Name:

What happened?

Date:

Location:

Prev session

Next session

So what?

Now what?

Name:

Date:

Location:

What happened?

Prev session

Next session

So what?

Now what?

Name:

Date:

Location:

What happened?

Prev session

Next session

So what?

Now what?

Name:

Date:

Location:

What happened?

Prev session

Next session

So what?

Now what?

Name:

Date:

Location:

What happened?

Prev session

Next session

So what?

Now what?

Reality denied comes back to haunt.

Philip K. Dick

Self-deception is being capable of seeing something but choosing not to. What are you deceiving yourself about?

Name:

What happened?

Date:

Location:

Prev session

Next session

So what?

Now what?

Name:

What happened?

Date:

Location:

Prev session

Next session

So what?

Now what?

Name:

What happened?

Date:

Location:

Prev session

Next session

So what?

Now what?

Name:

What happened?

Date:

Location:

Prev session

Next session

So what?

Now what?

Name:

Date:

Location:

What happened?

Prev session

Next session

So what?

Now what?

Minutes may seem as worthless as pennies until you add them up. Neither should be wasted.

Richelle E. Goodrich

What takes a lot of your time/effort? What impact/benefit does each item provide?

Plot all your endeavours (work, projects, clients, etc.) on the graph below.

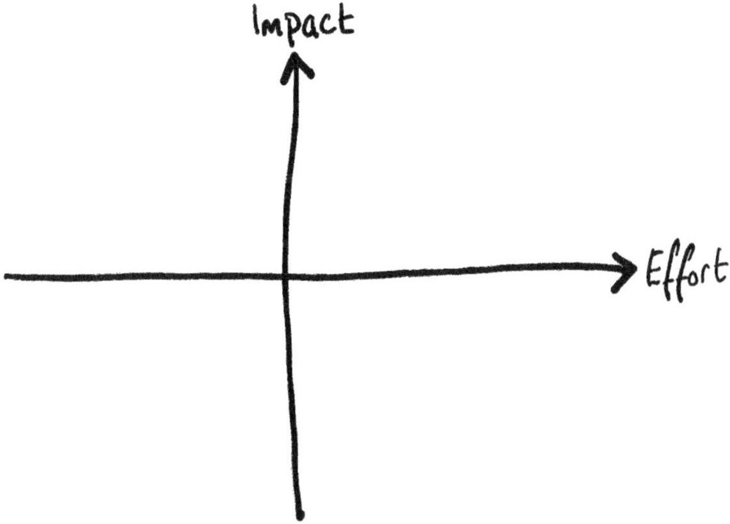

Which of those in the bottom right should you stop doing? How can you reduce the effort involved in all of the items on the right?

Name:

Date:

Location:

What happened?

Prev session

Next session

So what?

Now what?

Name:

Date:

Location:

What happened?

Prev session

Next session

So what?

Now what?

Name:

Date:

Location:

What happened?

Prev session

Next session

So what?

Now what?

Name:

Date:

Location:

What happened?

Prev session

Next session

So what?

Now what?

Name:

Date:

Location:

What happened?

Prev session

Next session

So what?

Now what?

When a person doesn't have gratitude, something is missing in his or her

Elie Wiesel

What three things are you grateful for in your life right now?

Name:

Date:

Location:

What happened?

Prev session

Next session

So what?

Now what?

Name:

Date:

Location:

What happened?

Prev session

Next session

So what?

Now what?

Name:

What happened?

Date:

Location:

Prev session

Next session

So what?

Now what?

Name:

Date:

Location:

What happened?

Prev session

Next session

So what?

Now what?

Name:

Date:

Location:

What happened?

Prev session

Next session

So what?

Now what?

I attribute my success to this - I never gave or took any excuse.

Florence Nightingale

What challenged you this week or is challenging you now?

What would you like the outcome of these challenges to be?

Name:

What happened?

Date:

Location:

Prev session

Next session

So what?

Now what?

Name:

Date:

Location:

What happened?

Prev session

Next session

So what?

Now what?

Name:

What happened?

Date:

Location:

Prev session

Next session

So what?

Now what?

Name:

Date:

Location:

What happened?

Prev session

Next session

So what?

Now what?

Name:

Date:

Location:

What happened?

Prev session

Next session

So what?

Now what?

I can see patterns in events, and behaviors; in mathematics, I follow slower.

Jacqueline Carey

What patterns in your coaching are you noticing?

ACKNOWLEDGMENTS

My appreciation goes to those who have helped create this book. Angie from pro_ebookcovers for the cover, Sandra from NounProject.com for the Cut image, Paul Lowe for his proofreading skills and Belinda Griffin at SmartAuthorsLab for her help in getting the book launched.

Many of the concepts covered in this book did not originate from my brain and have been influenced by other great authors. I'd like to especially acknowledge: Terry Borton; Gary Rolfe, Dawn Freshwater and Melanie Jasper; Mary Louise Holly; Sarah Stephenson; Christopher Johns; Graham Gibbs.

My family, again, has endured my tireless enthusiasm which I appreciate can be exhausting. Thank you for putting up with me and keeping me grounded. That includes you, Mr T.

Finally, thanks to Linda Spencer of Creative Vectors Ltd, Jiten Vara, Jim Wyllie, Rafa Ribeiro, Sarah Veall, Lucinda Quigley, my Oxford Brookes DCM crew, Tracy Avis, Louria Lindauer and AWA (Simon, Charley and Heather) who continue to be my partners in business, support network and generators of fresh perspectives.

ABOUT THE AUTHOR

David Lowe believes that everyone has the right to improve their work and personal life, so divides his time between coaching and training individuals, teams and organisations.

He has coached a variety of individuals and companies (ranging from start-ups to traditional organisations) over a range of industries (including retail, pharma, travel, health, fashion, wine, government, automotive and finance).

David has a post-graduate certificate in Business & Personal Coaching from University of Chester and is currently engrossed in a Doctorate in Coaching and Mentoring at Oxford Brookes University, researching the use of humour in dyadic coaching relationships.

Find out more about David at https://davidlowe.coach

ALSO BY DAVID LOWE

The Innovation Revelation: A story about how to satisfy customer needs

A real-world guide to taking a customer-focused approach to creating products and services that people actually want and are happy to pay for. A light-hearted fictional story, *The Innovation Revelation* follows Charlie Blades, a desperately unhappy IT professional struggling to survive in his job at one of the UK's top department stores. He is on the cusp of walking away from it all when he realises they've been doing everything wrong.

The Lemonade Stall: how to test and validate ideas

The Lemonade Stall comprises a short story and a suite of practical exercises to help you understand how to use the scientific method and hypotheses to achieve successful products and services.

The story follows many familiar characters from the highly successful *The Innovation Revelation* but twists it to a more practical application by asking you to consider how you might apply the methods, tools and techniques in your environment.

Scrum 101: The most frequently asked questions about Agile with Scrum

Based on real questions from real people in real talks, groups and workshops over many years, this book provides answers to the questions on Agile and Scrum that you want answered.

You're on Mute! Facilitating online workshops with a touch of fun

Seasoned facilitators, David Lowe & Rafa Ribeiro, have cooked up a handy guide to running entertaining workshops, including a tasty buffet of activities for you.

This is an essential guide for anyone wanting to create engaging, online workshops.

WHAT HAPPENED?

- What did you do and say? What did they do and say?
- What else did you notice? (paraverbal, non-verbal, expressions)
- What went well? What did not go so well?
- What did you want to happen? How did what happened differ from your expectations?
- What was your role?
- How did you feel? How do you think they felt?
- What did they want/need/expect from you?
- Was what you did appropriate? Was what they did appropriate?

SO WHAT?

- Why did you act in the way you did?
- How do your past experiences relate to what happened?
- What beliefs or assumptions were involved?
- How did your/their behaviour fit with your values?
- How have your views changed?
- What are the consequences?
- How do you feel about it now? Why do you feel like this?
- What other options did you have?
- What have you learned?
- What would you keep and what would you change?
- What else is going on?
- In hindsight, what do you think you should have done?
- So what does this mean to you as a person/as a coach?

NOW WHAT?

- What do you want to do about it?
- What is the plan?
- What is the first step?
- What is the timescale for your actions?
- What do you think will happen if you take those actions?
- What action do you need to take for other clients too?
- What is the right thing to do?
- What could you do differently if in the same situation again?

Printed in Great Britain
by Amazon

80015852R00093